Harriet,

God restores!

Isaiah 61:3

Jul R

Up from the Ashes

A Handbook for Healing

Jennifer L. Disney

iUniverse, Inc.
New York   Bloomington

Up from the Ashes
A Handbook for Healing

Copyright © 2010 by Jennifer L. Disney

Scriptures taken from the Holy Bible, New International Version®, NIV®. Copyright © 1973, 1978, 1984 by Biblica, Inc.™ Used by permission of Zondervan. All rights reserved worldwide. www.zondervan.com

Scripture taken from the NEW AMERICAN STANDARD BIBLE®, Copyright © 1960,1962,1963,1968,1971,1972,1973,1975,1977,1 995 by The Lockman Foundation. Used by permission

iUniverse books may be ordered through booksellers or by contacting:

iUniverse
1663 Liberty Drive
Bloomington, IN 47403
www.iuniverse.com
1-800-Authors (1-800-288-4677)

ISBN: 978-1-4502-5274-4 (sc)
ISBN: 978-1-4502-5276-8 (ebook)

Library of Congress Control Number: 2010913590

Printed in the United States of America

iUniverse rev. date: 11/22/2010

To my three boys
James, Denzel, and Derek,
and to my wonderful husband Eric

Contents

The Journey Begins

This morning, James is the first to arise. He is always the first one up. Unlike his little brother Denzel, he does not prefer to sleep in. He has always been this way. Growing up he had to get up early so I could take him to my mom's before I went to school and then to work. Thinking back on those days, I do not know how we ever got through it. He was such an amazing little boy. I do not know how I could have made it through life without my little man. In a way, James saved me from many years of pain. It was because I was pregnant with him that I stopped partying and started focusing on school and eventually on getting my teaching degree. When I found out I was pregnant, I almost ended his life to take care of the "situation," but somehow I found the courage to do otherwise.

I love our relationship. I am so close to him because of the many years that it was just the two of us. James shows his sensitivity by how he cares for his two younger brothers, Denzel and Derek. I love to watch all of them interact. I love to see James care for them. He was eight years old when I had Denzel, and he was mama's little helper. Even now when he has to go to baseball practice, he asks if I am going to be okay without him. What little kid thinks about anyone but himself?

I can now hear Denzel begin to stir. I walk into the living room.

Eric has already jumped in the shower. James is asking me when Eric is going to be ready so they can go out for their monthly ritual of "the guys' breakfast." I learned long ago that girls are not invited. I was both a little hurt and touched at the same time. Even though Eric is not James's father, they are very close. I met Eric when James was just six years old, and after dating and knowing we were going to get married, I introduced the two of them. They hit it off right away and have been buddies ever since. They have this special bond that I can't explain, and I am so thankful that they are close.

James walks into Denzel's room and carries him into the living room so they can watch cartoons together. They sit side by side on the couch, glued to the television. James has his arm around his little brother. I can now hear Derek starting to cry. I walk into his room, change his diaper, and take him to his two older brothers to join in on watching cartoons. With his free arm, James holds Derek, and as I walk away, I see Derek look up at his older brother and give him a big smile. My three boys are just sitting on the couch and enjoying cartoons on a Saturday morning. They all love each other so much. James watches out for Derek and Denzel. And the two younger ones love having an older brother to look up to.

If someone could look into this perfect scene, they would say how blessed this mom is to have three amazing little boys who love each other and look after each other. I wish I could tell you that this is how my life has turned out. I wish I could tell you that I watched all three of my boys grow and learn about the world, but that is not true. This is not the situation that came to be. I have been blessed with the reality of watching Denzel and Derek come into this world and grow. I have been able to hold each of them in my arms and kiss their soft cheeks. I was not able to experience those joys with James. He never made it into this world. His life was cut short before he was even born.

Part I

Chapter 1
The Day My Life Changed Forever

It was all I could do to keep it in. It was all I could do to go through life with the fear that someone was going to find out what I had done. So much time was spent trying to convince myself that I was doing the right thing. The list of excuses I came up with was incredible.

"This is my body."

"I did not ask for this."

"It was a mistake."

"It will ruin my future."

"What will my family say?"

"What will people think of me?"

If you are like me, you feel shame every time someone talks about abortion. I was worried that someone was going to discover my secret, and I carried it with me for years before I could open up and share my story with other women. I had convinced myself that the only way out of my situation was an abortion. It seemed so easy going into it, and our culture had normalized it so much that it seemed to be the best path. I ignored my other options.

No one made a big deal out of it, so I figured I must have been doing the right thing. Once I told my doctor I was pregnant, it seemed like this choice was the next step in the process. He knew exactly what to do, and he knew exactly who to call. It was even a fairly inexpensive solution. It was a small price to pay for a huge mistake. My friends at the time seemed so supportive. They were telling me that I was making the right decision.

"It is just a medical procedure."

"It is not even a child yet."

"No one is going to find out."

"No one should tell you what you should do with your own body."

So I set the appointment and the day slowly approached. When the day finally arrived, I got ready in a robot-like manner and left for the clinic. Upon arriving, I was confused and angered by the crowd outside of the clinic asking me to change my decision. In a daze, I walked inside and allowed the last attempt at changing my mind to vanish. There were no words spoken in the waiting room. I just silently waited to be called inside.

Once inside, the assistants explained the procedure, I signed a bunch of papers, and they got me ready. I am sure so much more happened, but those small details seem to escape me. I was escorted to another room to put my personal belongings inside a locker, and I waited. There were other women in the room, and it seemed so strained and quiet. One by one, we were called into the room and prepared for surgery. Then the staff gave me anesthesia, and that was the last thing I remembered.

The next thing I knew, I was being wheeled into another room. Next to me were women who had been called before me. One by one, other women who had had the same procedure were wheeled in after me. It was like a factory. The women all around me were so sad. Some were crying, some were like stones, and some were trying to act cheerful. Regardless of how they were acting on the outside, if they were like me, it did not cover the fact that they felt empty on the inside. The staff tried to quickly get us ready to go home because their lunchtime was drawing near. I got dressed and went home with the person who had brought me. It was on the ride home that I realized the pain of what I had done.

It was amazing how one incident affected how I viewed the world around me for the rest of my life. I was scarred so deeply, and no matter how much I tried to put a bandage on my wound, what I really needed was some major surgery. There were so many unexplained emotions that would spring up when the topic of abortion was brought up. I wanted to defend "my choice," but I did not have the nerve. I wanted to cry every time I saw a child who was the age my child would have been. I wanted to reach out to women who were contemplating abortion, but who was I to tell them not to go through with it? I had given in to the pressure myself. I felt I was being punished when it took me more than a year to get pregnant again. I constantly felt anxious, and I could never really put my finger on the cause of this emotion. Anger, fear, depression, shame, and so much more seemed to surface in my life at different times. When these feelings would come up, I would not know why I was feeling this way. Someone would say something that would make me feel like I wanted to share, but I was too ashamed to share anything. I could never reveal my true self because of what I had done. There was always that deep, dark secret.

What are some of the emotions that are springing up inside of you? How do you feel about what I have just shared with you? Please journal in the space provided.

I know the feeling of emptiness, and I know that there is freedom. God wants to release you from the bondage and give you that freedom. There is a reason this book has crossed your path. It is not a coincidence. Don't allow the worry and shame that someone will find out what you have done prevent you from continuing with this book.

You may be wondering why you even need to deal with your abortion. You may think, "If I am a Christian, then shouldn't the blood of Jesus cleanse me from all sin? Why do I even need this book to help me? God should be enough." And you are right, God should be enough. But it is human nature to be incapable of truly understanding the power and depth of God's forgiveness. We have a hard time forgiving ourselves and moving on. I bet that you have held this secret inside for a very long time. You were just praying no one was going to find out. You would be so amazed at how many women share your secret. Millions of abortions have occurred since *Roe v. Wade.* In fact, one in three women has had an abortion (Guttmacher Institute, State facts about abortion: New York, 2006). The chances that someone sitting next to you has had an abortion are very great. I hope you put your fears aside and finally allow yourself to feel and process the pain and damage done to your heart from that abortion. This book is a starting point for you to begin the healing process. This book will allow you to really understand how much abortion has damaged your soul and how God wants to take all of the pieces of your heart and put it back together again. This can happen because this book will help you to understand how much healing your heart really needs. I suggest you go through the book completely without skipping around. Healing is a process, so it is important to follow that process from beginning to end. Throughout the book, I have included different activities for you to complete. I know some of these may be difficult, but healing can be a difficult process. I would encourage you to give it a chance and to complete each step before moving on to the next.

At certain parts in this book, I refer to my son James, the child that I had aborted so long ago. Understand that as part of the healing process, it is important to pray for God to reveal the identity of your child, including the sex of your child and your child's name. This helped me realize that he was a real human being. This part of the healing process is not for your child; your child is already in heaven. This step is needed for the parent to have closure.

Once, during a powerful prayer time with a compassionate group of women, the Lord gave me a scripture through one of them. That scripture is the basis of this book.

> To appoint unto them that mourn in Zion,
> to give unto them beauty for ashes,
> the oil of joy for mourning,
> the garment of praise for the spirit of heaviness;
> that they might be called trees of righteousness,
> the planting of the Lord, that He might be glorified.
> Isaiah 61:3 (King James Version)

This book is a journey of healing through this scripture. The Lord guided me to write this book based on this scripture, and there is so much healing power in it for you. When researching the meaning of the original text in Hebrew, I came across so many enlightening definitions. I believe this verse maps out a process for women to follow that will allow them to heal from the pain of having an abortion.

To appoint unto them that mourn in Zion

The first part of the verse is a call to those who are mourning. Abortion brings on such a sense of loss. You not only lost a child, but you lost the child because of your choice. If you have not already done so, you need to allow yourself time to mourn the loss of that child. God is calling you to heal from this painful decision. The Hebrew word for "to appoint" means "call," "change," or "lay down." God sees your sadness and pain. He is calling you to change your thoughts and lay down that sin in order to have a healing in your heart. Now is the time for you to begin the process of healing.

To give unto them beauty for ashes

Throughout your life you have made choices, both good and bad. The bad choices have contributed to a pile of ashes that has slowly grown over the years. God wants to help us find the beauty in the ashes of our lives. These chapters will help you find that beauty once again and allow you to see yourself as God sees you.

The oil of joy for mourning

Once God has removed those ashes from your life, He wants to replace them with joy. There are so many things to be joyful for in our lives. This part of the book will help you to release mourning in your heart and to replace it with joy.

The garment of praise for the spirit of heaviness

There is so much fear associated with having an abortion. Usually, the greatest fear is the fear that someone will find out what you have done. When they do find out, we fear that they will judge us for our decision and think less of us. It is time to take that spirit of fear and turn it around to praise God for always being there for us. When we are at the height of our fears, we need to realize that God is always with us every step of the way.

That they might be called trees of righteousness,
the planting of the Lord, that He might be glorified.

A healed woman is a powerful woman. No matter what you have done, God can use it to His end and for eventual blessings for you. He will take this tragic event and use it for His glory. There will be a time you will stand before other women who have gone through the same experience and guide them in the healing process. God wants you to use your experience to make a difference in this world. The end result will be amazing, and God will be glorified throughout it all. I am so excited for you. Completing this process will bring more to your life than you ever expected.

Before you read the next chapter, I would like you to share your beliefs on abortion. How do you feel about it? Have your views changed over the years? If they have changed, how have they changed? Use the space below to share your beliefs.

_____

_____

_____

_____

_____

_____

_____

_____

_____

_____

Chapter 2
Is Abortion a Choice?

For many years, I believed that having an abortion was up to the woman. I grew up in a time when women were becoming stronger and bolder in the world. The age of the powerful woman had emerged in society. "I am woman, hear me roar" was a very popular motto for women of the sixties and seventies, and it seemed to be lived through the daughters of the eighties, nineties, and beyond.

In the past, women had felt so controlled by a society dominated by men that they were now taking back their pride with vengeance. No longer was it the norm to be a stay-at-home mom. The American dream now included a need for both parents to work. Women were not willing or were unable to sacrifice their careers to raise a family. They were handling both home and career. In fact, many women were choosing to bypass a family altogether in order to further their careers. Women often viewed children as a hindrance, especially because their careers were for themselves and, as is often the case for men, supplied their sense of worth.

This aggressive attitude in the workplace spread to the

social scene as well. Many women began taking charge of their relationships and sex lives. They were tired of men being in control, and they were going to take charge now. Many women became pregnant more often because they did not think about the consequences of their reckless behavior. Instead, they thought more about doing what they felt like doing. Repression was over!

A pregnancy turned into a minor "bump" on their journey to career success and was not going to stop them. *Roe v. Wade* made sure of that. This critical court case gave women the right to choose what they wanted to do with the children growing inside of them. Its proponents got it through the courts by claiming that having an abortion was every woman's constitutional right, that this decision was part of her "right to privacy." We made ourselves feel better about killing a child by saying all of these lies.

Unfortunately, some women found themselves at a very young age feeling all alone and too frightened to tell their parents that they were pregnant. Others were married at the time and did not want to have children at all, or they did not want to add to the number of children they already had. Still others were trying to make sure that the men in their workforce were not going to have a leg up because they didn't have to worry about getting pregnant. Women wanted an option so they did not have to end their self-centered ways of life.

I thought I was going to be a very powerful woman one day. I felt that I could do anything I wanted and that nothing was going to stop me from fulfilling my dreams. You'd think I would have prepared more since I was so set on my goals in life. But, like many people, I acted in the emotion of the moment, became pregnant, and thought about the consequences later. In order to allow myself to feel better, I listened to all of the lies and chose to believe them. Looking back on my life at that time, and the lives of so many women, I realize how much selfish thoughts can control our every move if we let them. Do you really think that you are making your own choice? There is a real battle raging inside each and every one of us, a battle between good and evil. The world tries to sell us the lies in a pretty little package called "choice," but there is a huge price you have to pay for this package. On the other hand, God wants to give you an absolutely free present, the gift of truth.

For so many years, I walked around blinded to all of the lies of this world. I listened to the lie that I would feel so much better if I would get high, thinking the drugs would help. I listened to the lie that I would feel more loved if I had sex with that man. And I listened to the lie when I got pregnant that it was my body and that I should have the choice to do with it as I pleased because there would be no consequences.

Women today cry for independence and for the ability to take charge of their lives. They are not in charge of their lives. They allow evil to speak lies to them and steer them down a path of destruction. If I am making you angry right now, it is probably because I am speaking truth to your heart.

If you think I am one of those women who always had these beliefs, you are wrong. One year I helped organize a Walk for Choice in Los Angeles. I went to the AIDS walk in Los Angeles to promote our walk. I was going to do everything in my power to make sure women had the right to choose to have an abortion. I thought it was best for them, unaware of the damage that follows. Unfortunately, I was not fighting the right fight. I was fighting for a life of entrapment. Do you think that God wants to control your every move because He is on some sort of power trip? That is not God's nature. He loves the people of this world, and He wants nothing more for you than success, to make sure that we become the best people we can be.

How long are you going to allow the devil to influence your decisions? I know a God who cares so much for me that He has mapped out a beautiful future, far more fulfilling than a life without Him. He has taken my destructive years and has used my hurts to help other women. My God gives me *choices* that bring wholeness and *guides* me in the right direction. There are really only two choices in this world: a life of peace and a life of chaos. Aren't you tired of living the life of chaos? Now is the time to choose the life of peace. God will take care of everything; you just need to trust Him. I am not saying it is always easy because it is not. But give God the chance to carry you through those difficult times and to rejoice with you during the times of joy. I can guarantee that you will have a life that is never boring, and when you die you will live with Him for eternity.

Chapter 3
How We Create a Life Full of Ashes

When I first read Isaiah 61:3, the part that spoke to me the most was, "To give unto them beauty for ashes." I think the whole concept about how beauty can come from ashes mesmerized me. How can something that has anything to do with beauty be produced from something as lifeless as ashes? Before we can explore this transformation process, we need to admit to those times in our lives when we have produced this lifeless dust.

You may think that it would be better to continue to try to forget about all of those bad choices you have made. But you and I know all too well that the enemy does not let us forget. There are so many areas of your heart that you have tried to close off and shut down, but God has other plans for your life. You see, the enemy loves secrets. If he can get you to hold onto those secrets just a little bit longer, then he can keep you in that bondage and prevent you from stepping forward.

At this point, it is very important that you begin to think about all of those shameful things you have done. The time in my life before I knew the Lord is the period during which I produced the most ashes. It seems that before we establish a relationship with God, we make so many bad choices, including sleeping around, doing drugs, and so on. These choices contribute to our ash piles. I believe that many people have lifeless areas of their hearts. When we are not following what God wants us to do, then we just continue to add ashes to the pile.

I know that you understand what I am talking about. You can feel that dead area of your heart. When I had my abortion, I created more lifeless ashes. I took them and I shoved them deep inside my heart so that I would not have to deal with them. I pretended that it did not affect me and that I did not have any reason to feel guilty. Why should I feel guilty about something that was my choice for my body? How dare anyone try to control me! I hadn't yet realized that I had chosen a path that would control me more than I truly understood. If you think about your situation when you set foot into that clinic, you may be amazed at how you were being controlled. Consider the process that takes place: You check in with a receptionist. You are called into a room to talk to someone about your finances. Another nurse checks your vital signs. You are then sent to another room to put your things in a locker. A different nurse takes you into an operating room with more new people around you. You are sedated for a bit so they can perform the abortion. Then you are taken into the recovery room, where another group of people try to quickly help you recover so they can move on to the next woman. You are never allowed to stay with the same person for very long. The clinic employees do not want you to develop any type of bond with one of the workers. They take you blindly through a maze of rooms and people so you will be so confused that changing your mind ceases to be an option.

We live in a society that has trained us to fight for our right to have choices. What we have truly been trained in is selfishness.

Women in this world are destined for this destructive life because of their "right to choose." They are being taught to make choices that are going to affect them for the rest of their lives. The truth is that once you get past the fact that it was your choice to abort a pregnancy, you realize that it was your choice to end a life, and then you have all of the ashes left to deal with. The shame forces you to hide them as best you can. These ashes you are left with smolder like an old campfire. They are still painful because they continue to burn inside.

All of the shameful acts are stuffed so deep that we think that no one is going to find them. Even if you have not told anyone, understand that there are at least three who know your secrets: God, Satan, and yourself. We have constant reminders of our "secrets"—every time we see a woman pregnant with a child and every time we see a child around the same age that our children would have been. And if you choose to have a child, just watching that child grow and develop reminds you that you were never able to watch that other child grow. Each time we are reminded of our shame, the feelings of anxiety and worry start up again inside our hearts. Whenever you have emotions that have not been dealt with, you can't make them disappear. They are always there, lying just under the surface and waiting for the chance to flare up again.

Do you know what frightens Satan more than anything? Taking all of those secrets and confessing them to our Lord and Savior, Jesus Christ.

> There is nothing concealed that will not be disclosed, or hidden that will not be made known. What you have said in the dark will be heard in the daylight, and what

you have whispered in the ear in the inner rooms will be proclaimed from the roofs.

Luke 12:2–3 New International Version

If you bring everything out into the open, then Satan has no power over you anymore. He can no longer scare you with the fact that he knows all of your dirty laundry. So here is what you are going to do. You are going to make a list of all of your secrets, and you are going to share them with God. Take comfort in knowing that He already knows. This is for your benefit. Eventually, you will find the courage to share them with someone else who is safe, but for now you are going to confess your sins to Him. When you are making your list, think of all of the things that have contributed to your ash pile. I have given you some space to write down your "ash list." If you have had more than one abortion, then you need to list each one separately.

List of items I need to confess (use additional paper if necessary)

1.	
2.	
3.	
4.	
5.	
6.	
7.	
8.	
9.	
10.	
11.	
12.	
13.	
14.	
15.	
16.	
17.	
18.	

Aren't you tired of producing ashes in your life? Aren't you tired of getting caught up in the same cycle over and over again? You need to confess all of your sins to God so you can get them out into the open, and the enemy will no longer have a hold on you. This is going to be your first step toward freedom from the pain. Now that we are aware that there is residue from our bad decisions, where do we begin the clean-up process? From here, we are going to discuss forgiveness. We are going to understand how to forgive ourselves and others. We are also going to see why it is so important to forgive.

Chapter 4
Finding Forgiveness

At this point in your healing, you should have completed your "ash list." The next major step in the process of healing is forgiveness. It is so important that you take this step to heart. We are going to cover two types of forgiveness in this chapter. First, you are going to need to forgive yourself for everything on the ash list. Most important, you are going to need to forgive yourself for any abortions you have had in the past.

The second type of forgiveness is the forgiveness of others. For whatever reason, we tend to have anger toward those who were around us at the time of the abortion. We are going to need to work through each and every person who needs to be forgiven, no matter how small their role was in the decision to abort your child. Even if you never told anyone about the abortion and sought no support, remember that there was a whole team of medical professionals who played a major role in your decision.

Forgiving Yourself

Let's begin with forgiving yourself. In order to do so, you need to remember where you were in your life at the time of the abortion. What circumstances were you in? How old were you? How much support did you have from those around you? How were you raised? How did you think this decision would affect you? In the space provided below, make a list of your circumstances or reasons you chose to have the abortion. Then check off each one when you confess the circumstance or reason and again when you ask for forgiveness.

Reasons for My Decision	Confess	Ask for Forgiveness
1.		
2.		
3.		
4.		
5.		
6.		
7.		
8.		
9.		
10.		
11.		
12.		
13.		
14.		

As for me, I was in my early twenties, not living the most honorable life, and I did not feel I could go to my parents with yet another disappointing mistake. I was not in a stable relationship, and I could not see myself with the baby's father in the future. I was in the middle of completing courses for a degree in chemistry, and I had a very busy social life that kept me out most nights. I was surrounded by people who did not seem to object to the fact that I was going to have an abortion; in fact, some encouraged it. While it may seem like a list of excuses, you and I both know that each and every item on our lists makes us feel guilty for what we did. Believe me, I understand that, to us, each time we remember the reasons we had the abortion, it is just another reminder of how selfish we were at the time.

It is now time for you to quit believing all of the lies you have been telling yourself. You need to realize that once you give yourself to God, your slate is wiped clean. It is as if you had never made those bad decisions in God's eyes. Once you've asked God for forgiveness, He is faithful in forgiving you. This is a fact that most women have a hard time believing. If you do not already have a personal relationship with Jesus Christ, then I suggest you read this sinner's prayer before you continue on.

> Lord, I know I am a sinner. Please forgive me for my sins. Thank you for dying on the cross for me. I ask that you come into my heart, and I will make you the Lord of my life. I know that if I were to die tonight, I would go to be with you in heaven. Amen.

Saying that you forgive yourself is not enough. You need to believe that you are forgiven. You are going to need to verbally confess your list aloud to God. Something happens when we hear with our own ears the things we have done. First, it forces us to acknowledge what we have done. Verbally confessing our sins also removes the power from the enemy. Once you have verbally confessed your list, you need to go through the list again and ask God to forgive you for each item.

I know that God's forgiveness may be difficult for you to fully grasp. You may feel that one day you will be forgiven when you have become a better person. When you have volunteered to teach enough Sunday school classes, helped set up and tear down at church, or placed enough money in the offering basket for enough Sundays, then you will be able to ask for forgiveness and truly believe you have received it. Let me remind you of a very important verse:

> This righteousness from God comes through faith in Jesus Christ to all who believe. There is no difference, for all have sinned and fall short of the glory of God, and are justified freely by his grace through the redemption that came by Christ Jesus.
>
> Romans 3:22–24 (NIV)

There will never be a time in your life when you are truly worthy of God's forgiveness. We have been losing ground since the fall in the Garden of Eden. But that does not matter to God. He gave His son so you can be saved and forgiven for all your sins. Take this verse to heart and understand that you need to have faith that God knows everything you have done and will do. He knows all of this, and He is still willing to forgive you and love you like no one else in this life could.

Forgiving Others

You may think that you should have no reason to forgive anyone else for your abortion. Why should you blame anyone else for your decision? But I know that I held resentment in my heart for people around me, and I needed to go through the process of forgiving them so I could move on in my healing process. For a long time, I blamed the boyfriend who got me pregnant. I felt that if he had stepped up to the plate, I would have never had the abortion. If he truly loved me, then he would have convinced me to keep the baby. The truth was that we weren't in a completely committed relationship to begin with. Neither of us were healthy enough emotionally to make the right decision.

As I began to go through the healing process, I realized that I held resentment for more people than I had previously thought. I thought about the people around me who had had abortions themselves. They never told me how emotionally painful it would be afterward. Maybe they were still numb to the pain because they never wanted to have to deal with it. And as I write this, I recall my own mistake in not trying to stop a close friend of mine from doing the very same thing, even though I knew how painful it really was. I think we try to ignore the fact that we hurt so much from it. We try to ignore the fact that we are damaged by it.

Another group of people that we need to forgive is the medical professionals we encountered when we were having the abortion. They have seen thousands and thousands of women go through this and know how women behave afterward, yet they never warn you. I am sure some of you were lying on that table and crying out, but they did nothing to console you. They did nothing but tell you that you were going to have to calm down. The mechanical reactions of the nurses and doctors made you feel like you were all alone and that you were no different from cattle being led to slaughter. Some of you may have believed that once you went beyond the waiting room there was no other option for you, no turning back. Abortion clinics make a lot of money every day. They count on the fact that you are not going to change your mind, so saving a child is like losing money. You went in to have it done, and they had been trained to make sure it was completed. In the table that follows, I want you to list all of the people you need to forgive and how they hurt you.

People I Need to Forgive	How They Hurt Me
1.	
2.	
3.	
4.	
5.	
6.	
7.	
8.	
9.	
10.	
11.	
12.	
13.	

Inside your heart right now, I am sure the feelings of anger and hurt are welling up. You feel that you were betrayed by so many people. It feels like something impossible to get past. Now is the time for you to give this pain over to God and to forgive those who were directly or indirectly involved with your decision. Now is the time for you to forgive your boyfriend, your friends and family, the medical team, and anyone else who comes to mind. Forgive them because you cannot go any further in the healing process until you do. Verbally say it out loud, confess your resentment to your Lord and Savior, and forgive those who were around you.

If this is something that you are having a hard time getting through, maybe you need to take some time to pray and ask God to help you forgive. Take a moment and think about all of the sins you have committed. God has forgiven you for each and every one. This is certainly a call for compassion. I pray you can find it in your heart to also forgive others.

Chapter 5
Find Your Beauty

*Instead, it should be that of your inner self, the unfading
beauty of a gentle and quiet spirit, which is of great worth
in God's sight.*

1 Peter 3:4 (NIV)

Once you have given your heart to the Lord, you will become
aware of an inner struggle between how God expects you to
behave and what the world expects. The world is telling us that we
need to voice our opinions. The world is telling us that we need
to stand up for what our culture believes to be "our rights" and
that we need to do whatever it takes to make ourselves happy. We
need to make sure that we are independent and take charge of our
own destinies. This might be your current mind-set.

God teaches us something different. Before you begin to
defend yourself and say how controlling God is, you need to
realize that it is not control; it is love. It is like a parent putting
parameters in a child's life for the child's best interest. God teaches

us that we need to lean on Him. He wants us to know that He has a plan for our lives. I don't know about you, but I find comfort in knowing that God is taking care of everything for me.

Therefore do not worry about tomorrow, for tomorrow will worry about itself. Each day has enough trouble of its own.

Matthew 6:34 (NIV)

With this inner struggle, we tend to take one of two paths. The first path leads us to a life of pain and shame. Most of us choose this one because we believe that this is the path where we have the control. We are going to do what feels right to us with little regard for consequences, and it does not matter what anyone else tells us. You may think that this path gives you great freedom, but I can tell you from experience that it entraps you more than you realize. I discovered this because I traveled this path for a very long time. It was on this path that I found myself in terribly unsafe situations.

I found myself doing things that slowly ate away at my beauty, and I'm not just talking about the physical. You see, the bad choices I made and the situations I put myself into just added to my hurt. I would do things that I knew were wrong, and yet I continued to do them because of my own selfishness. I was going to exercise my independence at any cost. The shame just continued to build, and every day I found myself looking in the mirror at someone I began to hate. I felt so ugly and dirty. My abortion just added to all of the filth. I felt like I was worthless. Even after giving my life to God, I still didn't feel pure and acceptable. I had to seek God and ask Him to show me my beauty.

One night at a singles retreat, I got down on my knees and

asked God to help me love myself again. When you ask, He will help. I lay on that floor, and I cried from the deepest part of my soul. I could feel God's arms around me, and I allowed Him to heal my heart. He took away all of the shame from my past. He helped me to know that when He forgave me, my slate was indeed wiped clean.

It was at this point in my life that the path I was on changed drastically. I began to see myself how God sees me. I truly began to love myself. I believe that women are amazing and beautiful creatures. We are incredible, emotional beings that have the ability to produce life. I know that so many women do not see how beautiful they are. They do not wake up in the morning, look in the mirror, and see how amazing they are. *You are beautiful.* Tell yourself that every morning.

By this point, you have analyzed your life and made a list of all of your ashes, and you have forgiven yourself and others. Now is the time to truly take it to heart and believe it. God sees your beauty, and He wants you to see it. Don't let your mind dwell on the lies that are being replayed in your mind over and over. Don't listen to your parents teasing you about eating too much. Don't listen to your friends on the playground making fun of your teeth, your hair, your height, or the size of your nose. Whatever lies you've been told, it's time to clean out your esteem closet. And every time these messages creep in, you need to shout, "I am beautiful!" This will not come easy. You have been thinking this way for a very long time. You are going to need to constantly remind yourself. Eventually, it will sink in and the negative messages will subside. In time, you will believe it when God whispers in your ear, "You are the most beautiful creature I have ever created. I don't care what you've done; I am so proud of what you have become."

In the space provided, make a list of all of the things you like about yourself and why you like them. Focus on these aspects of yourself every day.

What I Like about Myself	Why

Millions of women across the world have been affected by abortion and each has her own story. I represent only one of those stories. Now I would like to share with you another woman's journey and how abortion has affected her.

Pam's Story

I grew up in an intact upper-middle-class family. I am the oldest of four girls. I had always been the one to set the example for my siblings, and I held that position pretty well. During the summer between my sophomore and junior years in high school, everything radically changed. I met this guy who I thought was the answer to my dreams. You see, I had never felt like I fit in anywhere. I was very shy and insecure. With this guy paying all this attention to me, I felt I had finally arrived. I began to party. Drinking and experimenting with all kinds of drugs became a regular thing. Of course, in order to do all of this, I had to continually lie to my parents.

Eventually, I lost my virginity as well. Even in that, I felt it was a rite of passage and normal. No one taught me that I should value my body and that this decision would forever change my life. As is usually the case in teenage romances, sex became what our relationship was all about. It was all underground; I was completely going against everything my parents had wanted for me, and they didn't have a clue. This relationship started to get rocky within a year. At this time, I became interested in a guy who went to our rival high school. A group of my party girlfriends planned a trip to Palm Springs near the end of our junior year. We were all going to stay at this one resort, and a group of guys from the other high school would be there as well. Of course, I lied to my parents about where I was going and whom I would be with. I even lied to my boyfriend.

During one of the nights on this trip, I found myself passed out drunk on the hotel bed. The guy I thought was so cute knew he could take advantage of me. And he did. He rustled me up and into the shower. It was there that, I now realize, I was raped. In typical teenage fashion, I thought the next day, "Wow, aren't I something!" I never thought that what this guy had done was wrong. Instead, I lied to myself that he liked me. What a joke!

Reality set in when I missed my period the next month. Within a few weeks of that, I was throwing up every morning. My parents thought I had the flu. I was miserable and scared to death. A pregnancy test at a Planned Parenthood clinic confirmed my greatest fear: I was pregnant. There was no way I could tell my parents. Actually, I had no one to tell. So I did what I thought was my only choice. I told my boyfriend that I was pregnant by him and that he had to pay for me to have an abortion. In my heart, I knew who had gotten me pregnant.

Once my boyfriend agreed to it all, I made an appointment for the "procedure" as soon as possible. Back in the seventies, we were all under the false impression (or lie) that if you had an abortion before you were twelve weeks along, what was inside you was not a baby. I was probably at least ten weeks pregnant. I remember Mark picking me up and driving me to the Santa Ana Planned Parenthood clinic, and I walked in by myself with my boyfriend's hundred dollars to do the unthinkable.

I recall that after they took me back, the nurse said to me, "Because you are the tenth person in today, you get to have a special drug." *Wow, isn't it my lucky day*, I sarcastically thought. The good thing was that whatever they gave me completely knocked me out. Before I knew it, I was sitting in the waiting room. Mark took me home, in complete silence. I went into my house and decided to never think about what I had just done again.

In order to deny my feelings about the abortion, I became very reckless. I drank a lot, did a lot of drugs, became very promiscuous, and adopted an attitude of "I don't care." I really didn't care about anything, least of all myself. I just wanted to graduate, get out of Newport Beach, and start over in college. Thankfully, I finished my senior year, and I thought I could leave all of the bad memories and bad choices behind.

But abortion does not leave anyone unscathed. After more than thirty years of being in denial, the Lord forced me to take a look at what I had done and to go after my healing. Little did I realize that one day I would have an incredible ministry helping others to heal from their abortion experiences. It was awesome to not be afraid anymore. I had never wanted anyone to know, and I had always thought that I was going to be punished. The freedom of finally feeling forgiven was something I had to share with others. I am so thankful that I finally reached the end of myself and came clean with Jesus. He can do the same for you.

Part II

Chapter 6
Replacing Mourning
with the Oil of Joy

You prepare a table before me in the presence of my enemies.
You anoint my head with oil; my cup overflows.

Psalm 23:5 (NIV)

God has anointed us with the oil of gladness. Throughout the Bible, whenever someone was anointed with oil, they were to be set apart from everyone else. You may already feel set apart because you feel like no one could understand or accept you with all of the mistakes you have made in your life. You may feel your face warm with embarrassment every time you think about your past. When I say that you are set apart, you believe you are set apart for all of the wrong reasons. You are convinced you are not worthy to receive any good that God wants for you. There are so many women who are in your situation. That filthy feeling begins to creep back into your heart and you think, "How could God anoint me?" The true reason you are set apart is because you know you have sinned and you have asked for forgiveness. Now God wants to replace your mourning with joy. Let's examine two influential people in the Bible: Rahab and King David.

Rahab was a prostitute in the city of Jericho. Her occupation was well known throughout the city. When Israel was going to take over the city of Jericho, Joshua sent in two spies to check out the land. The city of Jericho was part of the promised land, the land God had promised to the Israelites. The spies went to Rahab, and she hid them from the king of Jericho even when he sent a message to her asking specifically about them. Rahab had heard about all of the wondrous miracles God had done for them, so she took a leap of faith and believed the men of Israel. She hid them in her house and lied to the king of Jericho about their whereabouts. When it was time to destroy the city, the Israelites remembered Rahab and spared her and the lives of her family. She was once a prostitute, but she ended up changing her character. Several generations later, Jesus came through her lineage. (If you are interested in learning more about Rahab, you can read her story in Joshua 2.)

Now let's take a look at our next example. In the Old Testament, King David was an anointed king. One night, while on his roof, he saw a beautiful woman, Bathsheba, bathing. He sent for her, and they participated in a sexual union. She became pregnant. In order to cover up his sin, he called her husband from the battlefront so that he would sleep with his wife and David would not be blamed for the pregnancy. Unfortunately, the husband did not sleep with his wife because he did not feel right having the comforts of home and his wife while the other soldiers were living in tents. So King David sent him back to the war, and he was killed on David's order. David and Bathsheba ended up losing the baby, but they did get married and have another child named Solomon. Solomon is one of the wisest men of the Bible, and he is also in the lineage of Jesus.

Throughout history, God has used men and women who might be considered unworthy in society's eyes. Since the time of Eve, women have been sinning. We live in a fallen world. Whether you feel like Rahab, the prostitute, or David, the adulterous king, your sin is no greater than those of anyone around you in church on a given Sunday morning. The secret that you hide from them is no different from the secrets that they hide from you. Understand that we are all damaged people. Yet, even with your sinful past, God wants to set you apart and use you to further His kingdom.

You are set apart and anointed because you are one of God's children. He brought our Lord and Savior Jesus Christ through the bloodlines of a prostitute and an adulterous woman. He sees all of His children as precious and set apart because they have given their lives to Him. God knew the path you would take. He grants us free will, so you were allowed to follow your path of choice. He knew before the world began, and yet He still set you apart from everyone else because you are special.

Before I formed you in the womb I knew you,
before you were born I set you apart;
I appointed you as a prophet to the nations.

Jeremiah 1:5 (NIV)

Have you ever noticed how those who come from royalty tend to hold their heads high? They seldom hang their heads in defeat. They have a certain confidence about them. Did you know that you are royalty? It is now time for you to take the position that has been ordained and walk with confidence.

Take this truth to heart and get rid of all of the lies the enemy has been feeding you all of your life. God has always thought of you as someone important. He has always "set you apart," and it is time that you believe it. It is time for you to rise from your pit of shame and take your place as one of God's chosen ones. Hold your head up high and take your place in God's royal family. He has had a place ready for you for a very long time.

Chapter 7
Healing Oil

I know that bringing up the terrible memories from the past has caused you to feel many emotions that you had shoved down deep inside your heart. I was really good at stuffing my pain, thinking that I could forget it. Now is the time to open your heart fully to the Lord and to allow Him to heal those wounds in your heart.

In the previous chapter I explained how God has set you apart as one of His royalty. Throughout the Bible, anointings were made with oil, which was also used in the church to heal people.

> Is any one of you sick? He should call the elders of the church to pray over him and anoint him with oil in the name of the Lord.
>
> James 5:14 (NIV)

Because of your abortion, the choices you have made since then have caused many wounds to your heart. I know that my abortion caused a huge wound in my heart, and it was only by God's grace and mercy that I was healed from that wound.

Now you may be thinking, "Why should I have to heal? What is the benefit of reliving this? I have dealt with it up to this point." Now, let's be realistic. I know there are times in your life when sadness suddenly overwhelms you. I am sure that you are silently suffering, and you are not ready to let go of that control. But that is not what God wants for you. He wants you to be healed. Don't just deal with it; relinquish it. It is time for you to allow God to explore all the chambers of your heart.

In order for the healing process to begin, you need to willingly give those areas of your heart over to God. Go back in time to the day when you had your abortion and when you took all of the emotions that you did not want to deal with and shoved them deep down inside your heart. You closed the door and threw away the key, or so you thought. It is now time to pray to the Lord, to ask Him to open up that door and begin to clean house. Don't be afraid. If you are, it's okay, but don't let fear stop you from doing what needs to be done. God loves you so much that He wants to take away that pain you are feeling.

It is so hard when you first begin the healing process because you feel like you are a constant spring of emotions. Once you have allowed God into your heart, He is going to begin to bring up many emotions that you have not felt in years. This is the time for you to mourn the loss of that child or children from so long ago.

Now is the time for you to think of them as real human beings. You need to realize that it is necessary to go through the grieving process that every mother who has lost a child goes through. This process can be pretty painful, but please follow it through. You will need to work through it in order to fully receive all God wants for you in this world. Here are the steps to the grieving process.

The first part of the process is denial, which may include numbness and shock. You may want to deny how much you have been damaged by this loss. This could be the part of the grieving process where you have been stuck for years. Now it is time to move on. Numbness may come first, allowing you to seemingly not have any feelings about the situation one way or another. Then the shock of it all settles in, and you feel the full impact of what has happened. And when you do, it will be like a floodgate has opened up. You may go through this time and experience difficulty holding your emotions in. That is okay. It's okay to allow some emotional time, as long as it doesn't become all consuming. Allow yourself to release all of it. There may be great help in support groups through your church or at a local Christian counseling center. Seek them out.

The next part of the process is bargaining. This is when you realize all of the options that you actually had and that would have been better choices than the one you made. Guilt and shame often accompany this step. It is so important that you remember that you have been forgiven and that God does not look down upon you. This is why you need to be able to forgive yourself. You are not the same person you were when you made that decision. God no longer sees you as a sinner because you have been forgiven. Since God has forgiven, isn't it time you consider doing the same for yourself? Although forgiveness is very important, hopefully you will never forget. One day you will be talking with someone who is struggling just as you have, and your experience will be exactly what she will need to hear about. You will be able to offer her hope.

The third part in the process may include depression. During this part, you may have a hard time eating and sleeping. You may begin to cry uncontrollably at times. It is often accompanied by feelings of emptiness, loneliness, and hopelessness. These are all normal responses. It is important that you fully go through this process so you can begin to get your life back on track. This is a normal purging process for the soul. When you are feeling depressed, sit before the Lord and pour out your heart to Him. He is right there with you. He is comforting you, and it is through this release of emotion that He can truly heal your broken heart.

The fourth step of the grieving process is anger. At this point in the process, you have cried, but typically you are still angry with others for the circumstance that you are in. You may begin to think of all of the people who directly or indirectly contributed to your decision, and you may be angry that they did not stop you from making the choice that you did. You may become angry with the doctors and nurses at the clinic for misleading you or your parents for not protecting you or your friends for being so supportive of the decision that has scarred you so. You may even be angry with God for allowing you to carry out the decision. "Why didn't he stop the situation, knowing it would bring me so much pain? Didn't he care about me? Wasn't I worth the effort?" It is time to acknowledge your anger; however, it is not necessary to seek revenge or restitution from those who may have contributed. This is a process for you to work through.

Finally, the last step is acceptance. This is when you accept the fact that you lost a child and begin coming to terms with what has happened. Not everyone reaches this step at the same time in the process. It may take some longer than others to reach this understanding.

The entire process may take a while, but give yourself some time. You may even go back to some of the early steps, but just continue and try to understand and accept the process. It does get easier with time.

It is so important for you to allow God's healing oil to seep through every part of your heart and do the work that it needs to do. You have been denying this process for so long, and the time has come to stop and go through the healing. Fully surrender yourself to God, and He will make the process as gentle as possible.

It may be very beneficial to find a good Christian counselor to help you facilitate this process. This book is only meant to help you get started and understand your need for healing. This process cannot be done alone. There is a reason God wants us to have fellowship with other believers. We can come together and share our feelings. It is important for you to get involved in support groups, Bible studies, and prayer sessions.

Chapter 8
Finding Your Joy

Your sun will no longer set, nor will your moon wane; for you will have the Lord for an everlasting light, and the days of your mourning will be over.

Isaiah 60:20 (New American Standard)

I know that it may seem like you are grieving for an eternity. You may feel that you are emotional all the time and you wish it would all end. I can assure you, my friend, that God will not allow you to grieve forever. He wants you to move on with your life. Just like it takes time for a wound to heal on your body, it takes time for your heart and soul to heal as well.

I remember doing all right for a while, and then all of the pain would rise up inside of me, and I would be overflowing with emotion. It was as if it had been there so long that it was compressed, and then it was like an explosion when I finally allowed it to come out.

You may have had an abortion and then the Lord blessed you

with more children. I thank the Lord for my two sons every day. Find joy in the fact that you are blessed with a child or children, a job, a place to live, and a car to drive. There will always be something in which you can find joy. It is so important that you find your joy in these things. We do not deserve anything that the Lord has blessed us with, but He loves us so much that He wants us to have it anyway.

In the circle below, I want you to list all of your joys in your life. In other words, how has God blessed you?

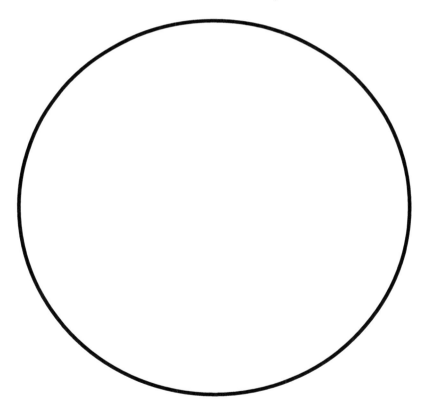

Now I want you to stare at this circle filled with God's blessings. While you are staring at it, I want you to remember the pile of ashes you have produced all of these years. Throughout our lives, we dump these ashes and make it hard for us to see the joys in our lives. We focus on the bad instead of the good. Now, imagine all of your ashes covering up your blessings. Then, I want you to imagine the breath of God blowing all of your ashes away so all you see are the blessings He wants to give you and has given you. Meditate on these verses of encouragement.

> When the Lord brought back the captives to Zion,
> we were like men who dreamed.
> Our mouths were filled with laughter,
> our tongues with songs of joy.
> Then it was said among the nations,
> "The Lord has done great things for them."
> The Lord has done great things for us,
> and we are filled with joy.
> Restore our fortunes, O Lord,
> like streams in the Negev.
> Those who sow in tears will reap with songs of joy.
> He who goes out weeping, carrying seed to sow,
> will return with songs of joy,
> carrying sheaves with him.
>
> Psalm 126 (NIV)

God is so good. He wants to restore the joy in your heart. I know that when He brings us through this healing process, He does it for our own good. When we come out the other side, we realize that we are better people for it. Find joy in the fact that you can wake up every day and know that you are loved by the creator of the universe. Find joy in the fact that God loves you so much that He sent His son to die for your sins.

When I was going through my postabortion Bible study, we watched a film called *Tilly*. It is an inspiring film about a woman who has an abortion. I was touched by the entire movie, but there was one scene with the mother and the child she aborted that really touched me the most. The little girl was sharing with her mother that Jesus came and played with her every day. I found that to be a comforting concept. Since the *Roe v. Wade* decision, 50 million abortions have been performed. The days on which they were aborted and the moments at which those children's lives ended, Jesus was there, waiting to usher them into heaven.

Ladies, I want you to find joy in all of these things that I have discussed. The most important thing for you to realize is that one day you will come face to face with your child, who is waiting for you in heaven. Rejoice, my sister, because one day you will hold your child in your arms. Rejoice, because on that day your child will not hate you or have ill feelings toward you; your child will just love you. In 2 Samuel 12, after David lost his child with Bathsheba, he explained to his servants that he would one day be with his child in heaven.

> His servants asked him, "Why are you acting this way? While the child was alive, you fasted and wept, but now that the child is dead, you get up and eat!"
>
> He answered, "While the child was still alive, I fasted and wept. I thought, 'Who knows? The Lord may be gracious to me and let the child live.' But now that he is dead, why should I fast? Can I bring him back again: I will go to him, but he will not return to me."
>
> 2 Samuel 12: 21-23 (NIV)

God is so good that one day we will be able to hold our children, stroke their hair, and love on them like we do our children here on earth. One day your children on earth will meet their brothers or sisters, and they will be able to hug them. It brings joy to my heart knowing that my sons will one day meet their older brother.

You see, the enemy has done a good job of trying to make you feel permanently condemned and ashamed for your bad decisions. However, God wants you to realize that you have been forgiven for all of your sins, and now He wants you to find joy in your life.

Now I present to you another powerful story about the experiences of a woman who has had an abortion. Lisa's story presents another set of hardships that she had to endure as a result of terminating her pregnancy.

Lisa's Story

I had an abortion (actually two) many years ago, and I never realized what it would do to me. You see, abortion doesn't make your baby "go away." That baby lives in your heart for the rest of your life. I was about nineteen years old and living with my boyfriend. I was working in a hair salon as a hairdresser, just beginning my career.

One day I realized my period was late. Up to then, I had always said that abortion was wrong, but really my beliefs were based on my Christian upbringing. Never had I done any research to find out the truth about how precious this little life really was. After I bought the pregnancy test, I woke up really early because somehow, I think deep inside, I knew. When I did the test, I sat on my bed looking into the bathroom, almost counting every second yet not wanting to know what I felt was probably true. I walked slowly to the place where my pregnancy test was, and the color was evident before I even could look down into the test results. *Positive!* Oh, no! I went back to the bed and sat there in shock. My immediate thought, without even a second thought, was, *I have to have an abortion.* My boyfriend was out of town, and I called him in tears. I don't believe that I told him at that time, but I felt so alone. I thought, *This should be a time that I can share this with someone, but I'm here all alone!*

Well, without getting into the rest of the details, about three weeks later my boyfriend drove me to the abortion mill. I went in, and he waited in the waiting room. I was crying so hard that I could hardly catch my breath. Deep down inside of me, I was looking for help, for someone to say, "You can have this baby and it will be okay," for someone to reach out to me instead of just watching me do something that I would regret for the rest of my life.

When I went into the back where all the other girls were taken, I was shocked at how many girls were there! Their ages seemed to be fourteen and up. Every single girl looked sad, depressed, and frightened. I wept and wept to the point that someone pulled me aside, and I talked to one of the head nurses in her office. Her words to me were, "You don't seem like you really want to do this. Are you sure about this?" My answer was not yes; my answer was, "My mom will kill me if she finds out and I'm afraid because I've started doing some drugs." She did not give me any positive options; she just said "okay" and let me go on.

After two hours of tests—urine sampling, blood sampling, and so on—I was put on a gurney in a room with four other girls, separated only by a curtain hanging on silver rings from the ceiling. The nurse came in, examined me, and coldly said, "You're eleven weeks." Then she moved on to the girl who was behind the next curtain and examined her, and so forth.

What I didn't realize is that my baby had a heartbeat, little hands, little fingers, and little toes. My baby sucked his or her thumb, and now that I know babies suck their thumbs because it is pleasurable, I also know they can experience pain.

When they rolled me out into the hallway, I was still crying, and the only kind touch that I remember during my experience was a doctor who came to me, leaned down, and whispered in my ear, "Dear, if you continue to cry like this, you will hurt much more after the surgery." Though that doesn't seem very caring, it felt like it to me at the time and it was the warmest touch I had had yet. I nodded my head and bit my lip to hold back any more tears.

When they rolled me into the prep room, they put me next to this beautiful young girl. She was next. We didn't say anything to each other. I remember looking over at her, and as she lay there, a tear rolled back on her face. They took her away, and I thought, "I'm next." It seemed like only minutes before they came and got me. They rolled me into a cold white room where all the staff was also wearing white, and the anesthesiologist leaned over me, put the mask on my face, and told me to count from ten to one. "Ten, nine, eight …," and I was out. I woke up on my stomach. Not only was I in physical pain; I was in emotional pain. I felt empty and alone. I no longer had my precious baby inside of me, the precious life that I wish I had today. His name was Vincent.

About ten years later (after my second abortion, Alicia), I met someone who changed my life. I fell in love with Him as He loved me through all of this, and He gave me something that I want to share with every woman who has gone through this horrible experience, no matter at what point in gestation they were. He showed me His love and His forgiveness. His name is Jesus Christ. The shedding of His blood cleansed me from my sin, from my shame, and from my sorrow.

Yes, we can try to go on and put away the pain of our bad choices ourselves, and we can also be angry at the people who didn't try to stop us, who could have at least said *something*. But anger and bitterness at others doesn't do anything but hurt us more than we already do. We need to learn to forgive as we have been forgiven. Also, I found that when trying to put the pain away by myself, I had to find other means to cover the pain and the guilt that I carried deep inside, the kind of guilt and pain that only a woman who has had an abortion can know. The means I chose were drugs, alcohol, and further promiscuity.

Truly, I have been set free from the pain and bondage of the guilt and loss of my babies. Don't get me wrong; I do think about them, and sometimes I think, "Where would they be today had I not made those wrong choices?" But the burn in my heart is no longer there. I will see them again in heaven. They know nothing but the love of our savior, Jesus Christ.

I have spent so many years trying to share with women going into these mills, trying to tell them what they may not have been told: there are other options. I also have spoken at different churches and events, sharing how wrong this choice is and that we need to further educate our youth so they know the truth. But even more important than that, I am able to minister and share the love, healing, and forgiveness that the Lord has given to me, and I am able to share that with hurting women.

If you are still hurting from an abortion you have had in the past, please just look up and ask Jesus to show you His forgiveness. Ask Him to come into your heart and clean out the pain, bitterness, and guilt and to take residence in your heart forever. He will come in and change your life.

Part III

Chapter 9
Eliminating Your Fear

For he will be like a tree planted by the water, that extends its roots by a stream and will not fear when the heat comes; but its leaves will be green, and it will not be anxious in a year of drought nor cease to yield fruit.

Jeremiah 17:8 (NAS)

Do you remember the cowardly lion in *The Wizard of Oz*? He was afraid of everything and everyone. He wanted to talk to the wizard and ask him to give him courage. I think many of us go through life frightened. We walk around pretending that we have it all together when, deep down inside, many of us are afraid of what is around the corner. I know I was. I am an excellent actress when it comes to my fearful attitude, but I was always afraid of what the future would bring.

It seems that when I had my abortion, I was afraid of so many things. I was afraid of what it was going to do to my body. I was afraid that I was making the wrong decision. I was afraid that my parents were going to find out. I was afraid that I was going to get pregnant once more and need to do it all over again. You name it, I was afraid of it. The abortion seemed to give me an extra layer of insecurity. I had yet one more dirty little secret to hide from the world. My life was this web of secrets. I could not even remember who knew which details about my life. Life became extremely exhausting because it was hard to keep up with all of my secrets.

When I became a Christian, I confessed my sin to God and He forgave me. That was so awesome. But I then began to have fear grow inside of me that the other women in the church were going to find out about my past. What would they think if they really knew me? I began to work through those fears after hearing the testimonies of other women. God kept bringing me women who had situations similar to my own. I felt more and more comfortable sharing my past.

Testimony is a powerful tool. The enemy does not want you to use it because he does not want you reaching out to other people. Communion and sharing with others were designed by God to mature us. These tools allow us to realize that we are not the most disgusting people in the world. Testimony helps us to see that everyone makes mistakes. It can also remind us of what we are capable of without God in our life. We begin to realize that once we share our past with other people, it dissolves the power of the fear that used to grip us. We no longer feel alone in our journey.

Once I began to reveal my past to other people in the church, I felt a new sense of freedom. I could share freely with other women and, more often than not, my testimony helped other women with their shame and their fears. I remember giving my testimony at a women's tea. After it was over, a woman from my church came up to me and said how touched she was by my sharing. She could relate to my story because she too had had an abortion.

So you may think that I had reached a point in my life where I had finally overcome my fears. The enemy does not let us off of the hook that easily. He will only try to attack us from a different direction. And he did find many places linked to my past where he could cause me to fear the future.

I met a wonderful man, and things seemed to be going very well for us. I finally felt like I was past all of my fears. My life really seemed like it was on track. I was so confident that I knew what God had planned for my life that I began predicting exactly when I was going to get pregnant. The running joke with my friends and family was, "I'll be pregnant by Friday." I was so sure that this was what God had planned for my life. I had thought it all out and knew exactly how everything was going to happen. But I had problems getting pregnant when we decided to have a child. We tried for about a year without success. Deep down inside, I felt that I was being punished by God because I had chosen to end my first pregnancy so many years ago. Each month when I would start my period, I would cry out to God and ask Him to forgive me over and over again. It was almost as if I was grieving the child that I had lost all over again. I had to realize that God is not like that. He loves us regardless of our past, and He wants to bless us even though we may not deserve it.

I eventually did get pregnant, but what if that has not been the case for you? Realize God is not punishing you. Sometimes what we want for our lives is not what He has planned for us. We need to come to a place of acceptance that God's will for us is infinitely better than our own selfish desires. We may need to give up our own desires so that we can receive God's will for our lives. We need to focus more on the blessings that God has given us rather than mourn our desires that He has not fulfilled. We need to trust Him and know that He has our best interests at heart.

When I finally had my first son, the enemy came at me with a new fear. I kept thinking that we were going to receive some news from the doctors about our son and that either he was going to die or something was going to be seriously wrong with him. I could not get past the fact that God could take him away from me at any moment. Again, deep down inside, I felt like I was going to be punished for past mistakes. I believed I didn't deserve to be happy.

Having an abortion seems to instill in our hearts this deep-rooted fear. The enemy sees this weakness and uses it to attack us daily. When we begin to work through each fear, he tries to find something new that is going to make us fearful. I look back on my life and the struggles I had with fear, and I can identify the attacks now.

I find comfort in the fact that I serve a God who sees my future and knows how each and every part of my life is going to turn out. It took me a long time to understand, but I finally realized that I need to turn that fear into trust. We have a phenomenal battery of ammunition to throw back at the enemy every time he tries to make us fearful. We have the word of God. It will help us fight our battles.

> In addition to all this, take up the shield of faith, with which you can extinguish all the flaming arrows of the evil one. Take the helmet of salvation and the sword of the Spirit, which is the word of God. And pray in the Spirit on all occasions with all kinds of prayers and requests. With this in mind, be alert and always keep on praying for all the saints.
>
> Ephesians 6:16–18 (NIV)

With each fear the enemy throws at you, throw scripture right back at him and trust in the Lord. Throw Jeremiah 17:8, from the beginning of this chapter, back in his face. I do not know where you are in your personal journey, but I do know that God does not want you to live like this anymore. He wants you to allow Him to help you use this strategy to work through the fears that are deeply rooted inside of your heart. The next two chapters are going to help you overcome the attacks of the enemy. With praise and prayer, I know it will only make your faith in God stronger.

Chapter 10
Breaking Down the Walls with Praise

The Lord is my rock, my fortress and my deliverer;
my God is my rock, in whom I take refuge.
He is my shield and the horn of my salvation, my stronghold.
I call to the Lord, who is worthy of praise,
and I am saved from my enemies.

Psalm 18:2–3 (NIV)

We learn at a young age that people can hurt us. Most of the time it is not intentional, but we live in a fallen world and no one is perfect. When we are born, we do not come with a set of instructions. Our parents make mistakes, and these begin to lay the foundation for the wall around us. I know that I will make numerous mistakes with my own children. This is not an issue for blame. We all come through life with wounding. Certainly our growing-up years are not the only influences that affect us. They are just the beginning. Each time we are hurt, we begin to go into a defensive mode and try to protect our wounded hearts.

We slowly add brick after brick to our protective wall until we no longer allow anyone to get inside our hearts to hurt us anymore. The painful things that I had done to myself, and that were done to me, made a great foundation for my wall. All of the shameful things I had done in my life added to the fortress, and I was very good at making sure my wall was never compromised.

There were so many emotions and so much pain that came along with my decision to abort my child. It was emotional overload, and I did not know what to do with it. From the moment I left the clinic, I could feel this pain inside of me, but I was so good at stuffing my emotions that I did not allow myself to feel anything for very long. I quickly numbed myself and added more bricks to the unending wall by getting back into my party life so as not to think about it.

When I became a Christian, I continued to fortify the wall. I tried so hard to guard myself from any pain. But God had other plans for my life. He wanted to help me break down that barrier and allow the healing to begin. One way this occurs is through praise and worship. I believe that road to healing can begin in God's house. The journey can begin when we worship God and allow the Holy Spirit to do the work that needs to be done.

We attend a church where it is not unusual to walk into the sanctuary, hear the band playing, and see people lifting their hands to God. I know that I truly love this time with God. I feel so close to Him when I am surrendering all and allowing myself to truly enter worship. At times when I would enter His house, something would be bothering me, but the moment the guitarist began to strum, I would break down. It was as if it penetrated the walls I had spent so much time building.

I love the intimacy of imagining myself alone with God, when it is just the two of us. I come into His inner chamber, and I sing to Him the many reasons I love Him and tell him how much.

God is so good that He sends His warming love back to me, and I can feel it rising up inside of me. It is as if I can feel my love tank being filled for the days to come.

How can we expect to get healing in our lives if we do not allow our hearts to be touched? How do we expect to move on in life if we do not learn to trust God?

The book of Joshua is such an amazing part of the Bible. It describes the time when the Israelites were beginning to fight for the promised land. God sent one of His angels to tell Joshua what He wanted him to do in order to conquer Jericho. They were to march around the city wall once each day for six days. On the seventh day, they were to march around the city seven times while the priests were blowing their horns, and then the people would shout and the walls would come tumbling down. If you take that step to trust God, this is exactly what can happen for you.

Doesn't this sound appealing? Won't your worshipping and shouting to the Lord help your walls to crumble? Perhaps it is impossible for anyone to get inside of your heart. You may think that people have tried before, but it was just too painful to let them in.

The next time you go to church and the music begins, make a decision to surrender to God. Allow Him to finally break down that wall and let the healing process begin. It's time to release that pain and break your cycle of denial and self-protection.

If it seems too hard to allow yourself to do this in a public place for the first time, find a good worship CD and pray to God to soften your heart. Allow Him to do all of the work. I am going to be honest with you—initially, it will seem that you are never going to stop crying. Remember, do not fear. You can trust that God is by your side, and He is there to help you begin to heal. Tears accompany healing. Remember that Isaiah 61:3 promises us that the result will be a "garment of praise for the spirit of heaviness."

Chapter 11
Bringing Your Broken Heart to the Lord

And pray in the Spirit on all occasions with all kinds of prayers and requests. With this in mind, be alert and always keep on praying for all the saints.

Ephesians 6:18 (NIV)

In our church, I am fortunate enough to have access to an anointed prayer team. This is a group of men and women who gather together and pray for the people in the church. They offer prayer after service, prayer times for the different ministries, and individual prayer by appointment for more extensive issues. It is truly outstanding how God has worked through these individuals to change the lives of so many people.

I have been fortunate enough to have this prayer team pray over me on several occasions. Coming away from each session, I know that God used them to speak to me and to help me in my future plans. It is important for everyone to experience the power of God through prayer.

You may be wondering why anyone would need someone else to pray for them. Scripture says I can pray directly to God myself. Scripture also states that there are times in our lives when we need someone else to agree with us in prayer. There is power in communion and prayer with others. The support of other believers can give us the boost we need to get the healing process started. There is also benefit in sharing your struggles with trusted others. Our darkest fears and secrets lose power when exposed to the light. Sometimes there are things that we cannot see because we are too close to the situation. A prayer time, guided by the Holy Spirit, can speak directly to our broken hearts. We may not know what to pray for, but there are prayer warriors out there who are sensitive to the voice of God, and they can speak to your soul even if you are inexperienced in such things.

When going through this healing process, it is going to be important that you have prayer. A good balance between group prayer and individual prayer is the best recipe. Do not rely fully on one or the other because God sanctions the intercession of others and also loves the one-on-one communion with you. Whether you go to a group of prayer warriors or you sit alone before God, it is essential that you understand a few basic principles about prayer.

1. **Do not think you have to be perfect before you can come to God in prayer.**

So many people avoid praying because they do not believe they are worthy. They think that they have made too many mistakes in their past or present. Just because you did not pray yesterday or last week does not mean you are not worthy to go to God and spend time with Him now. Do you cut off friends because they have not called you in a week? Hopefully not. Don't let your feelings of inadequacy get in the way of being blessed by God.

Many people do not think they know how to pray. It is just like a conversation with an old friend. Just sit and share everything that is in your heart. To get started, it may help to acknowledge God for who He is. Tell Him how important He is to you and why. Thank Him for all of the things you have received. That alone will have you talking for a very long time.

2. **Ask God to reveal any sins in your life and confess those sins to Him before you pray, and ask Him to forgive you.**

This will clear your mind and allow God to speak to your heart. It is like starting with a clean slate every time you approach God. This will help to relieve any guilt you may have. You don't need to feel embarrassed or ashamed when you share with God. Remember, He already knows what you have done and thought because He was with you. Your verbalizing it helps you take responsibility.

3. **Quietly sit before God and listen to what He has to say to you.**

Often we ramble on and on to God, and we do not give Him the chance to speak to our hearts. Realize that God is going to speak to you, if you let Him. He will probably speak to you by landing thoughts in your mind. The earth is not going to shake while the voice of God bellows out to you in your living room. It is so important that we quiet ourselves before the Lord and try not to busy our minds with our day. Eliminate the noise around you. Silence the cell phone, turn off the television, turn down the radio, and turn off the iPod. Be still; be silent. If we are distracted, we may miss God's voice.

After the earthquake came a fire, but the Lord was not in the fire. And after the fire came a gentle whisper.

1 Kings 19:12 (NIV)

4. Trust that the Lord has spoken to you.

Don't allow yourself to accept doubt. Your initial reaction may be, "That wasn't God; that was me." Silence the lies. Trust that God wants to have a personal relationship with you and believe that He is the one speaking to you. This is where faith comes into play. God does speak to us, and we need to trust in that. Listen to His promises because He always fulfills them. They may not come in our timing, but He is always faithful.

5. Always thank God for prayers that are answered and prayers that are unanswered.

We do not understand how God works. We may think that He is not listening to us because some of our prayers seem to go unanswered. Know that God is always listening to us. Sometimes we need to realize that those things we request may not be the best for us. What we want may not be what we need. God knows what we need in our lives before we even ask for it.

I can't stress enough the impact of prayer. It is a powerful tool God has given us to use in our lives. God can help us through this healing process in our times of prayer. I used to feel as if I were a caged animal with no way out. I was starting to "freak out" because I felt so trapped. In healing through prayer, God released me from that bondage and now I am free. Notice I said "free," not "perfect." I know you will probably begin by coming to Him for prayer specifically in regard to your abortion, but God wants to release you from so much more. Give God the chance to help you get progressively released from your bondage.

Part IV

Chapter 12
What Is the Next Step
in the Healing Process?

That they might be called trees of righteousness, the planting
of the Lord, that he might be glorified.

Isaiah 61:3 (KJV)

Let's review the process in this book. We first acknowledged
that we have made mistakes in our lives. These mistakes have left
us with lifeless ashes that leave a residue on many other areas in
our lives. It is important to forgive ourselves and others for the
mistakes that have been made. From this ash pile of our mistakes,
only God can bring beauty. We must ultimately accept the fact
that God made us.

Next, we looked at how we have been set apart from this world
by God. We are His chosen ones, and we need to realize that He
has anointed us to do great things. We need to allow God's "oil
of gladness" to heal our wounded hearts. Through that process,

we can find joy in our lives. We can now identify all of the great blessings for which we can be thankful.

Finally, we looked at the "the garment of praise for the spirit of heaviness." Some of us have a root of fear growing inside of our hearts. Since the abortion, we have not been able to accept the truth that we deserve to be blessed by God in spite of our mistakes. This fear can be erased from our hearts when we worship and praise God. Just like the walls of Jericho, God is going to use the music of worship to break down the walls that we have built. Prayer is another important tool to be utilized to get past the fear in our hearts.

So what do we do with all of this information? Where do we go next? I want you to know that when you fully heal from the pain of your abortion, God is going to open all kinds of doors for you. You see, now God can use you to help other people who have gone through the same process. You will no longer be afraid to talk to someone about your past. You never know when your testimony is going to touch the life of someone else.

I thought the end of this verse was so incredibly powerful: "That they might be called trees of righteousness, the planting of the Lord, that he might be glorified." What was meant for evil, God can use for good. During a forest fire, the plants and trees are destroyed, but not long after the fire a plant or tree will begin to grow up from the ashes. This perfectly describes how God can work in our lives. Only God can bring life from ashes. From the destruction in our lives, God can bring life.

In order for a plant to grow, it needs sunlight. Jesus, the light of the world, can come into your dark life to heal you from the pain and shame of your past.

When Jesus spoke again to the people, he said, "I am the light of the world. Whoever follows me will never walk in darkness, but will have the light of life."
John 8:12 (NIV)

In the beginning was the Word, and the Word was with God, and the Word was God. He was with God in the beginning. Through him all things were made; without him nothing was made that has been made. In him was life, and that life was the light of men. The light shines in the darkness, but the darkness has not understood it.
John 1:1–5 (NIV)

Whether you were a teenager finding out from a home pregnancy test in the bathroom at the mall or an adult taking a test in your home, when you finally told your doctor your decision, he or she did not have a problem with it. Or maybe you did not see your doctor at all in fear that your parents would find out because you were pregnant at such a young age. Everyone has her own list of circumstances that led to the abortion. My story is only one of millions. In addition to my testimony, you have read the stories of two other women.

Now that you have read my story and the testimonies of other women, what is your story? Use the space provided to write down what you had to go through and the circumstances that surrounded your abortion.

_____

_____

_____

_____

_____

_____

_____

_____

_____

_____

_____

Now that you have written your testimony, it is burned in your heart. This powerful tool will be used to glorify God as you complete your healing process. Something that you guarded as an ugly, shameful secret will be used to reach out to other women. This book was meant to help you begin the healing process. It is now time for you to reach out to a biblical counselor or support group or to participate in a postabortion Bible study. This book has crossed your path for a reason. God wants to bring light into your darkness.

When I think of trees, I think they symbolize strength. Throughout the process, you will grow stronger. You are in a spiritual battle, my friend. We need to stand strong and come together to help other women make the right choices. We need to be courageous and share our stories when the opportunity arises and reach out to other women so they can find freedom through forgiveness, healing, prayer, and praise.

As women, we are a powerful force. Fight for the future children of unwanted pregnancies. Throughout the Bible, there are stories of women who came from shameful pasts, and God used them for some of His most precious tasks. The basis of our Christianity is the fact that Jesus died on the cross for our sins. He was the ultimate sacrifice. He was without sin but came through the lineage of sinners. That should give you hope. Just as I have, you can be given the gift of healing. This is a truly precious gift.

I have a picture in my mind of my three boys, James, Denzel, and Derek. They are sitting side by side on the couch watching television together. Derek is in James's arms, staring not at the picture on the screen but into the face of his oldest brother, smiling from ear to ear. My middle son, Denzel, is sucking his thumb and resting his head on James's shoulder. This picture in my mind reveals a trio of brothers that will look out for each other and love each other always.

I know that I will not be able to experience the pleasure of seeing this here on earth. I hold onto the promise that one day Denzel and Derek will meet their oldest brother and will have the chance to love him. I also know that I serve a faithful God. He is so faithful and forgiving that I, too, will see James in heaven, and he will not hate me for what I have done. He will love me and be so very glad to see his mama. When you had that abortion, God ushered your child into heaven. God grieved for you and the pain you would endure from that day forward. That pain doesn't have to last forever. God bless you on your journey.

Postabortion Resources

Abortion Recovery International Network,
http://www.abortionrecoveryinternational.org

Cochrane, Linda. *Forgiven and Set Free: A Post-Abortion Bible Study for Women.* Baker Books. ISBN-13: 978-0-8010-5723-6

The Justice Foundation, 8122 Datapoint, Suite 812, San Antonio, Texas 78299, 210-614-7157, info@txjf.org, Project: Operation Outcry, 210-614-7157, 8122 Datapoint, Suite 812, San Antonio, TX 78229, http://www.operationoutcry.org

LIFE International, http://www.lifeinternational.com

National Helpline for Abortion Recovery, 866-482-5433

Silent No More, http://www.silentnomoreawareness.org/resources

Notes

Notes

Notes

Notes

Notes

Notes

Notes

Notes

Notes

9 781450 252744